Meet NASA Inventor Jonathan Sauder and His Team's

Clockwork Venus Rover

WORLD BOOK

www.worldbook.com

World Book, Inc.
180 North LaSalle Street
Suite 900
Chicago, Illinois 60601
USA

For information about other World Book publications, visit our website at www.worldbook.com or call 1-800-WORLDBK (967-5325).

For information about sales to schools and libraries, call 1-800-975-3250 (United States), or 1-800-837-5365 (Canada).

Produced in collaboration with the National Aeronautics and Space Administration (NASA).

Library of Congress Cataloging-in-Publication Data for this volume has been applied for.

Out of This World
ISBN: 978-0-7166-6261-7 (set, hc.)

Clockwork Venus Rover
ISBN: 978-0-7166-6265-5 (hc.)
ISBN: 978-0-7166-6281-5 (pf.)

Also available as:
ISBN: 978-0-7166-6273-0 (e-book)

Staff

Editorial

Director
Tom Evans

Manager, New Content
Jeff De La Rosa

Writer
William D. Adams

Proofreader/Indexer
Nathalie Strassheim

Graphics and Design

Senior Visual
Communications Designer
Melanie Bender

Media Researcher
Rosalia Bledsoe

Acknowledgments

Cover	© Mark Garlick, Science Photo Library/Getty Images; Jonathan Sauder	26-27	ESA/J. Whatmore/NASA/JPL-Caltech
4-5	© Droneandy/Shutterstock	28-29	Jonathan Sauder
6-7	© David A, Hardy, Futures: 50 Years in Space/Science Source	31	© Firehouse Horology
		32-33	© Triff/ Shutterstock
8-9	© Mark Garlick, Science Photo Library/Getty Images	34-35	Jonathan Sauder
10-11	NASA	36-37	© Shutterstock
12-13	Jonathan Sauder	38-39	© Mattel; Jonathan Sauder; Tyvak/Jonathan Sauder/ NASA/JPL-Caltech
14-15	NASA/JPL	40-41	NASA; Jonathan Sauder
17	© Oleg Yakovlev, Shutterstock	43	Kristine Berza & Oskars Berzs, LTD KOB ART/ www.kobartdesign.com
18-19	NASA		
20-21	© Mark Garlick, Science Source	44	Jonathan Sauder
23	National Maritime Museum (licensed under CC BY 2.0)		
24-25	Horology (licensed under CC BY 3.0); Public Domain (Daderot)		

Contents

Glossary There is a glossary of terms on page 45. Terms defined in the glossary are in boldface type that **looks like this** on their first appearance on any spread (two facing pages).

Pronunciations (how to say words) are given in parentheses the first time some difficult words appear in the book. They look like this: pronunciation (pruh NUHN see AY shuhn).

Introduction

When it comes to the planets of our **solar system,** Earth's next-door neighbor is Venus. At its closest approach, Venus passes within about 26 million miles (42 million kilometers) of Earth, about 10 million miles (16 million kilometers) closer than Mars ever comes. Yet dozens of **orbiters, landers,** and **rovers** have been sent to study the Martian surface. By comparison, the surface of Venus remains virtually unexplored.

For conventional **probes,** Mars is just an easier place to visit. The Martian surface may be cold, dry, and dusty, but it is a virtual paradise compared with conditions on Venus. There, the surface is hidden by thick clouds—including clouds of sulfuric acid. Beneath the clouds, the pressure of Venus's **atmosphere** is enough to crush a conventional spacecraft. And, it's hotter than an oven—hot enough to fry spacecraft electronics.

Extremes of heat and pressure have made the exploration of Venus's surface virtually impossible. The few **landers** that have reached the surface managed to continue functioning for only a couple of hours. And no **rover** has yet tested its mettle against the tire-melting temperatures of the Venusian surface.

The **engineer** Jonathan Sauder is looking to change that. Sauder and his team are working to develop a rover capable of exploring the **solar system's** harshest surface. To succeed, they will have to try some novel ideas—like powering the craft using springs and wind. The clockwork rover they envision may more closely resemble a wind-up toy than the tech-heavy robots that have explored the Red Planet.

Artist's illustration of Venus's surface

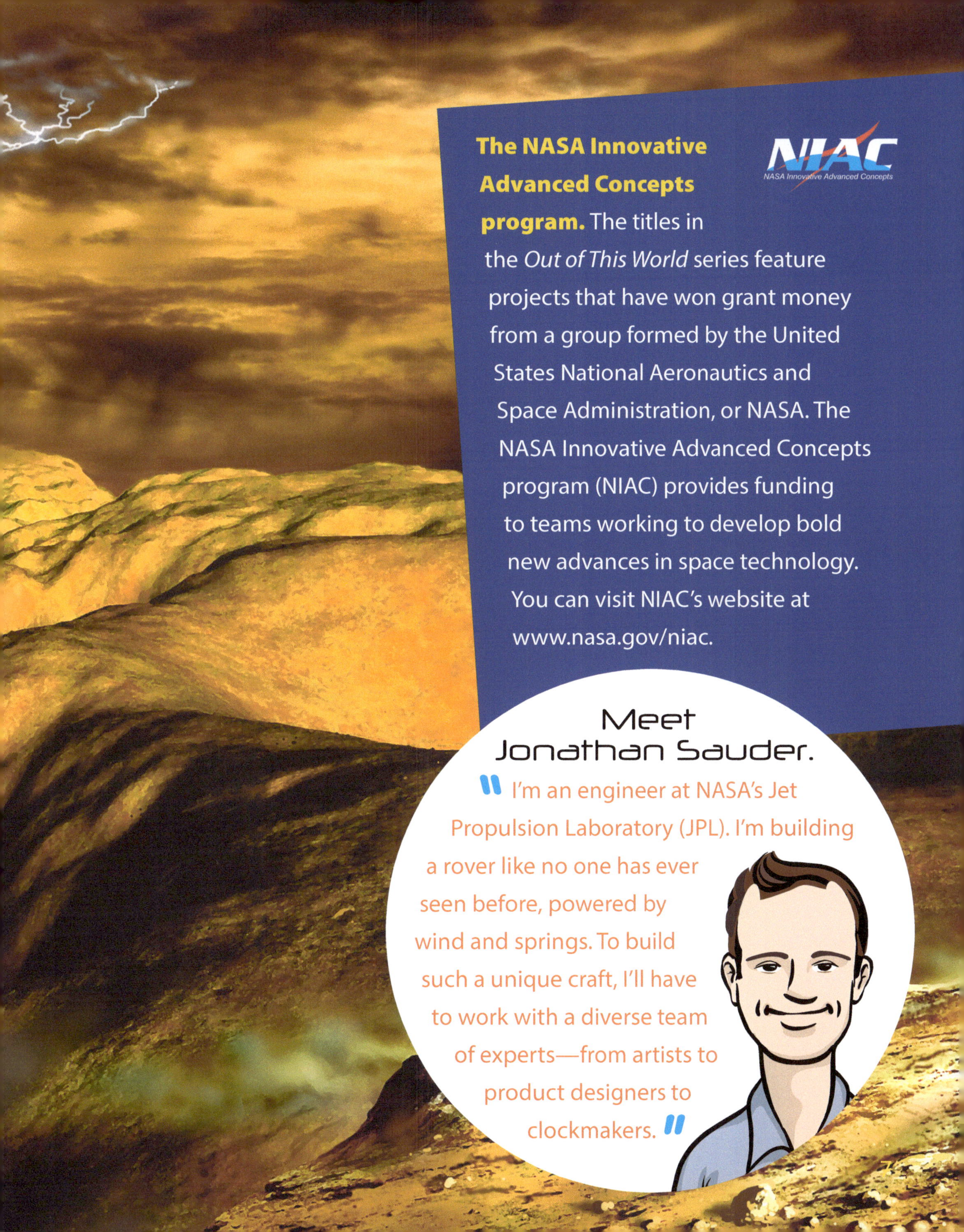

The NASA Innovative Advanced Concepts program. The titles in the Out of This World series feature projects that have won grant money from a group formed by the United States National Aeronautics and Space Administration, or NASA. The NASA Innovative Advanced Concepts program (NIAC) provides funding to teams working to develop bold new advances in space technology. You can visit NIAC's website at www.nasa.gov/niac.

NIAC
NASA Innovative Advanced Concepts

Meet Jonathan Sauder.

I'm an engineer at NASA's Jet Propulsion Laboratory (JPL). I'm building a rover like no one has ever seen before, powered by wind and springs. To build such a unique craft, I'll have to work with a diverse team of experts—from artists to product designers to clockmakers.

Earth's evil twin

Venus has an atmosphere even thicker than Earth's. The planet's surface is completely shrouded from view by swirling yellow clouds. Over the years, this has led people to wonder what lay hidden below. Up through the 1950's, even some scientists believed that lush jungles and swamps teeming with life might lie beneath the clouds.

Starting in the 1960's, the United States and the Soviet Union sent **probes** and **landers** to study the planet. (The Soviet Union was a nation that included Russia and nearby countries.) When these craft were able to pierce the clouds, they found a barren, hellish world.

Venus is the hottest planet in the **solar system.** Most of its atmosphere is **carbon dioxide,** a gas present in trace amounts in Earth's atmosphere. On Venus, just as on Earth, carbon dioxide helps trap the sun's heat, warming the planet. But Venus has much more carbon dioxide. As a result, its surface temperatures reach a blistering 870 °F (465 °C).

The thick atmosphere also produces a crushing air pressure on the surface—more than 92 times that of Earth. The **surface pressure** is equivalent to the pressure about a half-mile or almost a kilometer deep in Earth's oceans—enough to crush most submarines! The atmosphere is also corrosive, with sulfuric acid vapor hanging at the surface.

Why study Venus?

The daunting conditions make Venus hard to study. The searing temperatures cause electronic components to overheat. The Soviet **lander** Venera 13, launched in 1981, set the record for survival on Venus. The craft was able to operate on the surface for 2 hours and 7 minutes. This far exceeded its planned mission duration of 30 minutes. But it became difficult to justify sending expensive spacecraft to Venus just to have them burn up after an hour or so. NASA instead focused on Mars in its quest to study *terrestrial* (Earthlike) planets.

Why return to Venus? There are many important questions about the planet that remain unanswered. Studies have found that Venus was much like Earth for many millions—or even billions—of years after its formation. Like Earth, it likely had liquid oceans and more moderate temperatures. What caused Earth's twin to

turn into such an inhospitable wasteland?
Could the same thing ever happen to Earth?

Recent studies have determined that
Venus had Earthlike conditions at
a time when life was forming on
Earth. Simple life forms may thus
have arisen on Venus, too. They
could have died out when
the conditions worsened. Or,
just maybe, microscopic life
could have retreated into
the **atmosphere,** where
temperatures are cooler.

Astronomers have already begun
the search for **exoplanets**—planets
outside our **solar system**—capable
of harboring life. We already know lots
about Earth and a good amount about
Mars. Exploring Venus will help scientists
better understand terrestrial planets and
identify which exoplanets might hold life.

Sauder was inspired to pursue engineering by his grandfather, John Klotzle.

He was one of the people who really sparked my interest in inventing and creating and building and designing things, even though he didn't have an extremely technical background. —Jonathan

Sauder's grandfather was not an engineer, but a *line worker* for a telephone company. (Line workers build and maintain telephone and

Sauder and his brothers worked on many projects with their "Grampy."

power lines.) In his spare time, however, he was always tinkering and inventing things in his workshop. He passed his interest in inventing and a fascination with airplanes to his grandson.

Sauder spent much of his childhood working on his own inventions. He would build them with toys, kits, or anything else he could find.

Like many scientists and engineers his age, Sauder loved Legos growing up. Today, he even uses them in a class at the University of Southern California as a hands-on teaching tool. Students are shown and create well-designed mechanisms using Lego gears, axles, and bricks.

Starting from scratch

Sauder eventually set his mind to an ambitious task—designing a **rover** for the surface of Venus. A stationary **lander** can only study the surface from a single spot, but a rover can move around and gather information from many places. The rover is far more difficult to design and control, but it produces a richer study of the planet.

NASA has sent several rovers to Mars. All have been fantastic successes, operating far longer than planned and vastly increasing our knowledge of the Red Planet. But Sauder could not simply copy their designs. The environment of Venus is vastly different from—and more challenging than—that of Mars. So, Sauder set out to design a rover from scratch.

But Sauder still relies on the experience of those who designed the Mars rovers. For example, he has worked

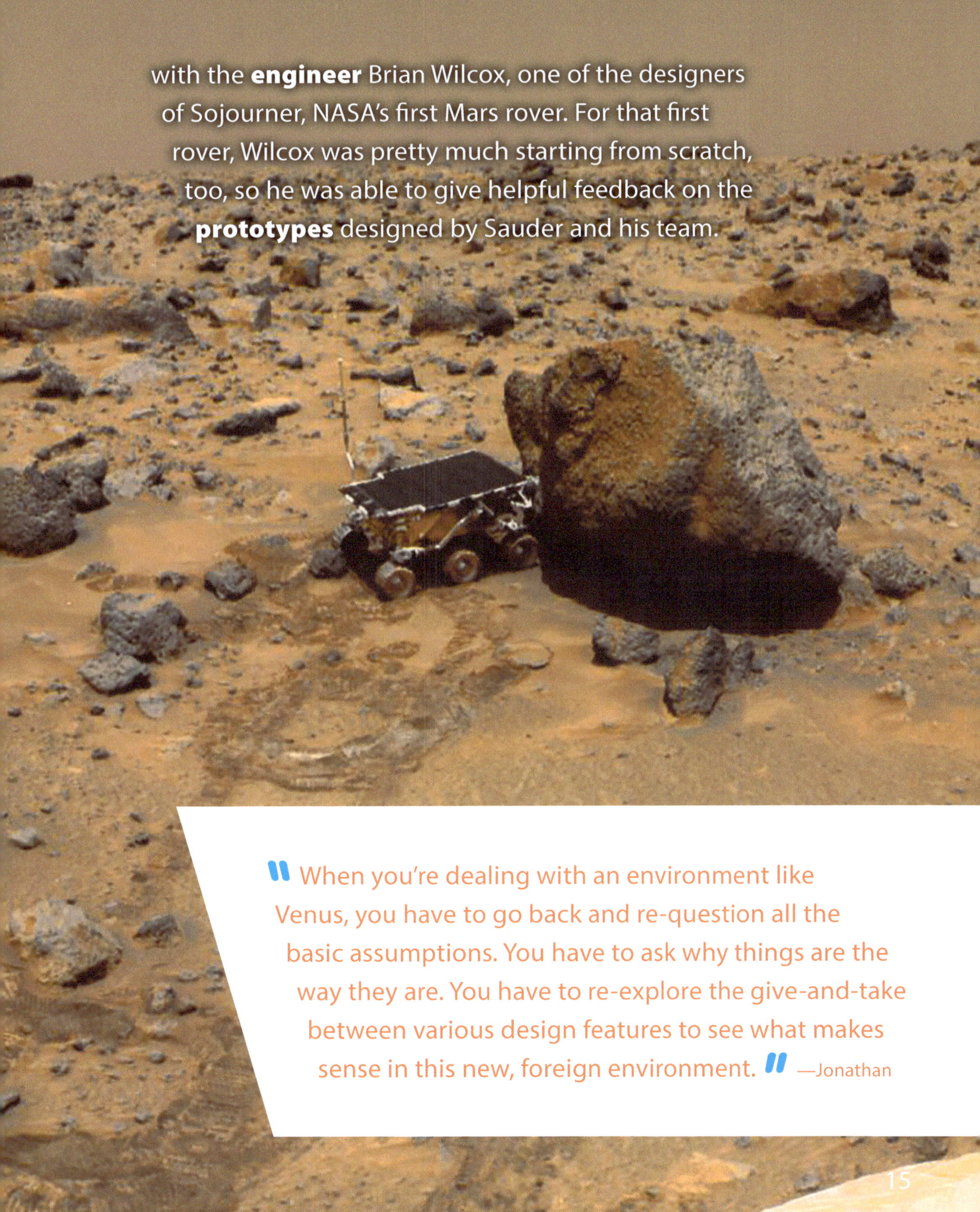

with the **engineer** Brian Wilcox, one of the designers of Sojourner, NASA's first Mars rover. For that first rover, Wilcox was pretty much starting from scratch, too, so he was able to give helpful feedback on the **prototypes** designed by Sauder and his team.

Inventor feature:
Entrepreneurship and space

Sauder attended Bradley University in Peoria, Illinois, to study **aerospace engineering.** But he soon became more interested in product design and *entrepreneurship*. An *entrepreneur* is a person who organizes and manages a business or industrial undertaking. An entrepreneur takes the financial risk associated with starting a business. Entrepreneurs earn the profit if the company succeeds, but they lose money if it fails.

Sauder was also interested in how people come up with new ideas, both individually and in groups, and how those ideas could be made into useful products.

❝ By working together, how can engineers stimulate new thought processes in one another that would generate new creative ideas? ❞ —Jonathan

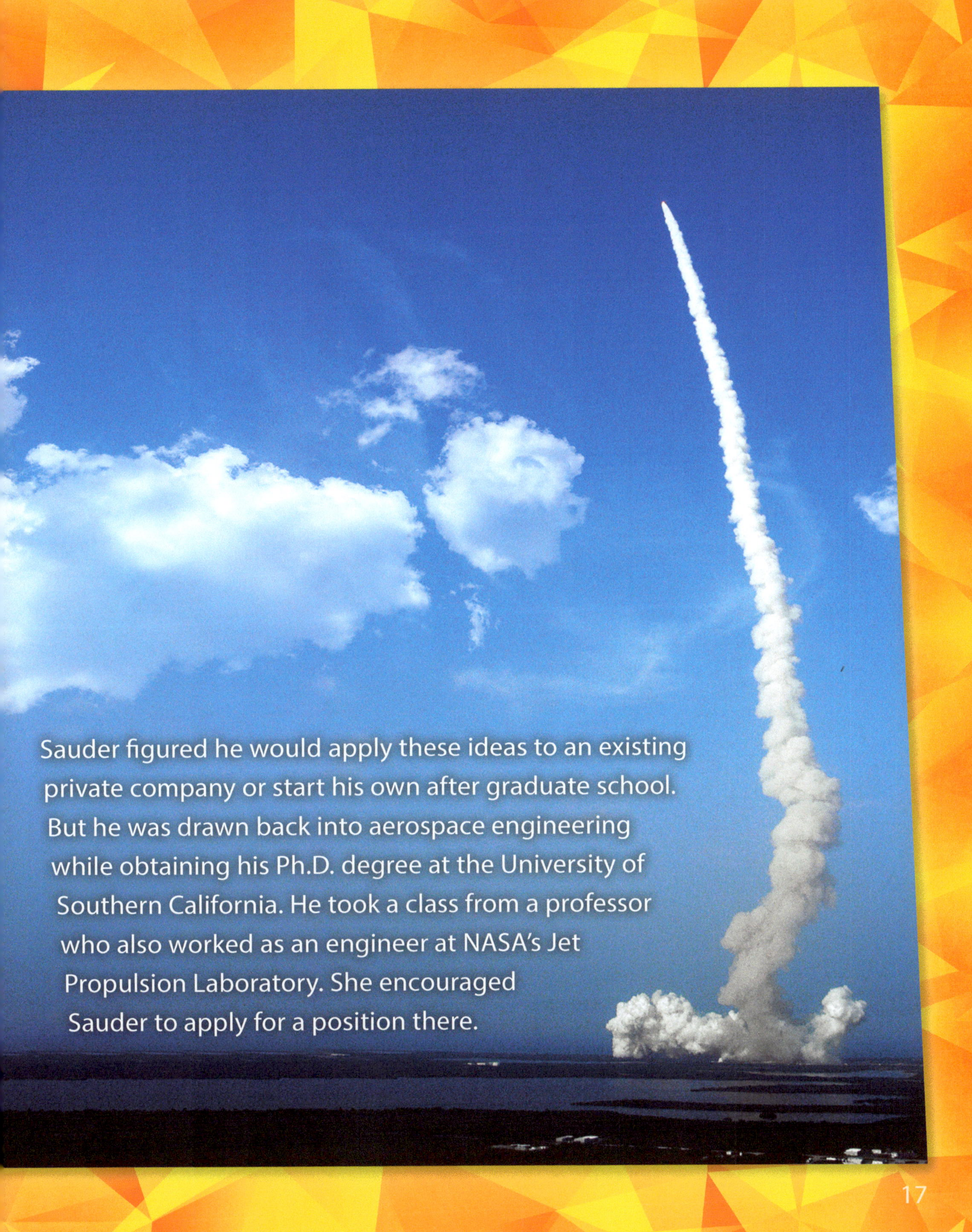

Sauder figured he would apply these ideas to an existing private company or start his own after graduate school. But he was drawn back into aerospace engineering while obtaining his Ph.D. degree at the University of Southern California. He took a class from a professor who also worked as an engineer at NASA's Jet Propulsion Laboratory. She encouraged Sauder to apply for a position there.

The limits of power

All **probes** require power. Many **orbiters** and **landers** make use of solar power. Sunlight can provide enough power to run an orbiter as far away as Jupiter. And, the closer you get to the sun, the more power solar panels can provide. Venus **orbits** closer to the sun than does Earth, where we use solar panels all the time. So, it would seem like a no-brainer for a Venus **rover** to make use of solar power.

In fact, there are several problems with using solar power on Venus. First, cloudy skies block most of the sunlight. Less light reaches the surface of Venus than that of Earth, even though Venus is so much closer to the sun. A rover would thus need a large array of solar panels to gather enough power. Also, the intense heat on Venus would melt traditional solar panels, so they would have to be made of specialized, heat-resistant materials. Such panels are less efficient at collecting energy.

Venus's orbital characteristics impose another problem. The planet rotates lazily from east to west. As a result, a full day-night cycle is 117 Earth days long! That means a rover would be without sunlight for about 60 Earth days and in twilight for another 15 Earth days on either end.

A rover would need massive solar panels and powerful batteries to gather and store enough solar energy to operate through the long, hot Venusian night. Otherwise, mission controllers would have to shut the craft down and hope it survived the punishing conditions until daybreak.

Where solar energy will not work, **probes** often make use
of radioisotope thermoelectric **generators** (RTG's). These
devices contain radioactive materials. Such materials decay
(break down) over time, releasing energy in the form of
radiation. RTG's use this energy to generate electric power.

RTG's can provide constant power for many years. But
like many things, they do not work well in the extreme
temperatures on Venus. RTG's are also incredibly expensive
and hard to make. Powering a Venus rover with an advanced,
heat-resistant RTG—if one could be developed—would likely
be too expensive.

Sauder realized he would have to come up with a novel
power source for his Venus rover. He looked to the planet
itself for inspiration.

Wind speeds at the surface of Venus average about 2 miles
(3 kilometers) per hour. On Earth, such gentle breezes
wouldn't be able to power much of anything. But Venus's
atmosphere is much thicker, so the winds blow with much
more force. A 6-mile- (10-kilometer-) per-hour wind on
Venus would feel like a gale on Earth!

Sauder and his team designed a special wind turbine to
power the rover. The turbine can be folded up for launch
and deployed once the rover lands. Its blades are specially
designed for the low-speed, high-density winds of Venus.

Artist's illustration of Venus's surface

Big idea:
Clockwork technology

Sauder's turbine could provide enough energy for the **rover.** But the high temperatures on Venus would make it extremely inefficient to generate electricity.

> **"** If we have a wind turbine connected to an electrical **generator,** and then have that generator connected to motors, we're going to lose about 90 percent of that energy due to the generator and motors working very inefficiently at Venus's high temperatures…The big idea here is that we take that wind energy and directly drive the rover. **"** —Jonathan

The wind turbine would turn a shaft leading down into the body of the rover. From there, gears could transfer the power to the drive system. Energy could even be stored mechanically— no batteries required. At windy times, excess power could be used to wind a spring inside the rover. When the winds die down, the spring would unwind to keep the rover moving— just like a wind-up toy! This type of mechanism, with gears driven by springs, is called a **clockwork.**

Sturdy clockworks

We know that clockwork mechanisms can be designed to stand up to rough conditions. Until the 1700's, sailors had no way to precisely calculate their longitude—their location east or west on Earth's surface. The problem was so great that the government of England, which had many overseas colonies at the time, offered a huge cash reward to anyone who could solve it. The English clockmaker John Harrison developed a sturdy clock that kept precise time even in the challenging conditions at sea. Such a clock is called a *chronometer.* A ship's chronometer was set to the time of the port from which it departed. Sailors compared the time on the chronometer with the local time—calculated by the location of the sun—to determine their longitude.

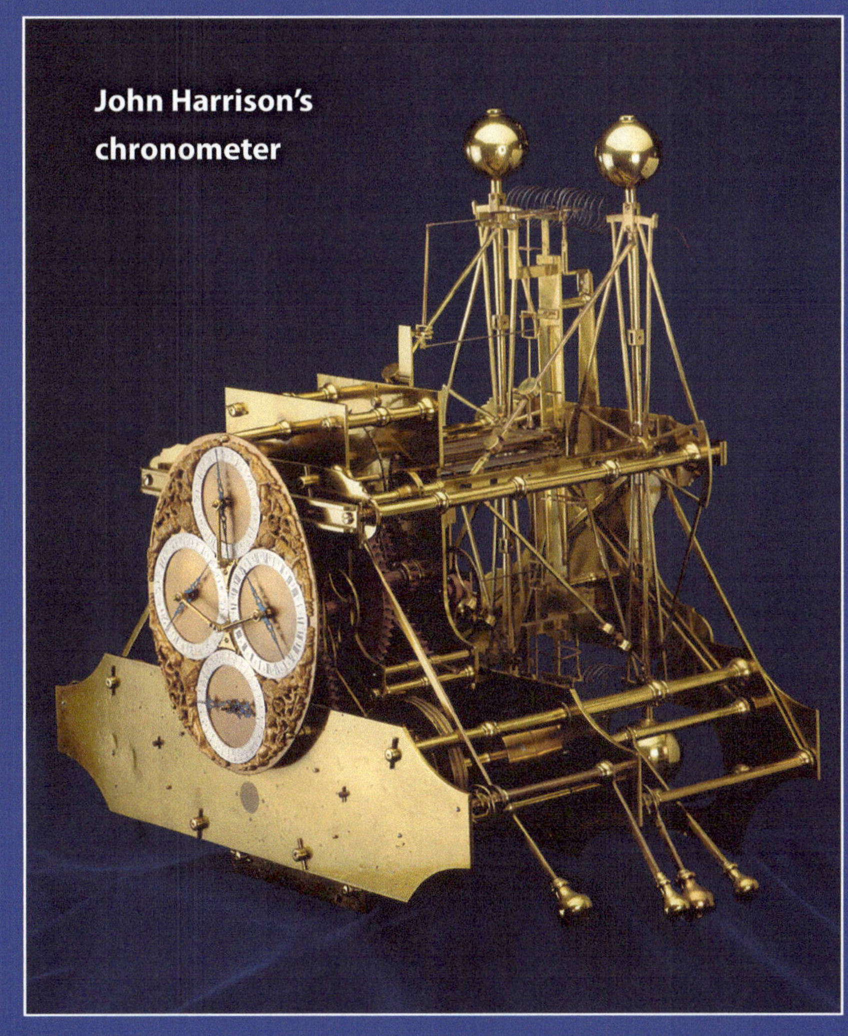

Automatons

Sauder calls the **rover** he's designing the Hybrid Automaton Rover-Venus—HAR-V, for short. But what is an automaton?

By the 1700's, clockmakers had the technology to create tiny gears, springs, and weights and assemble them into clocks that could be kept on a table or even in a pocket. But some of these skilled craftspeople created more than just clocks using clockworks. Inventors built delicate devices in the shapes of people or animals that moved as if they were alive. Some could dance. Others could write. Some could play music. These machines were called automatons.

Automatons entertained and amazed audiences and served as expressions of their inventors' skill and artistry. Many were incredibly intricate. Some could even be reprogrammed, for example, to play different songs—a hallmark of the modern computer. All of this was accomplished without electricity or any power source other than hand-cranked springs or weights.

Far left, an automaton clock from the 1600's. Left, this automaton, built around 1800, could be programmed to write sentences or sketch pictures.

Prototype: Venus walker

What should a **rover** look like? Should it have six wheels? Eight? Four? Should it even have wheels at all? The first HAR-V **prototype** had legs!

Sauder was inspired by the work of the Dutch artist Theo Jansen *(TAY oh YAHN sehn)*. Jansen creates amazing *kinetic* (moving) sculptures that walk using only wind power. He calls these creations *strandbeesten,* Dutch for *beach beasts*. (Jansen designed them to scuttle along beaches.)

> **"** We brought in Theo Jansen as an expert on intelligent mechanical systems. **"** —Jonathan

Sauder was already determined to use wind power, so he thought it might make sense to pursue a strandbeest-like design. Also, like legged animals, legged robots can move through all kinds of **terrain,** even going where wheels cannot. This ability could be useful on the surface of Venus, which might be littered with craggy rocks and pits.

However, Jansen advised against using mechanical legs like those of his strandbeesten. For legs to step on or over obstacles, they need complex control systems. Strandbeesten, by contrast, have an ingenious, but simple,

Sauder's first designs for a Venus rover had legs, as seen in this illustration.

design. Their legs have no way to adjust their stride to handle obstacles. A sizeable rock or hole can even topple a strandbeest. Legs that could handle obstacles would need electric motors and electronic **sensors**— exactly what Sauder was trying to avoid.

Prototype:
Venus tank

Sauder next considered moving the **rover** with treads, like those of a tractor or tank. At the front of the rover, the treads would angle upward, enabling the craft to climb over rough **terrain.**

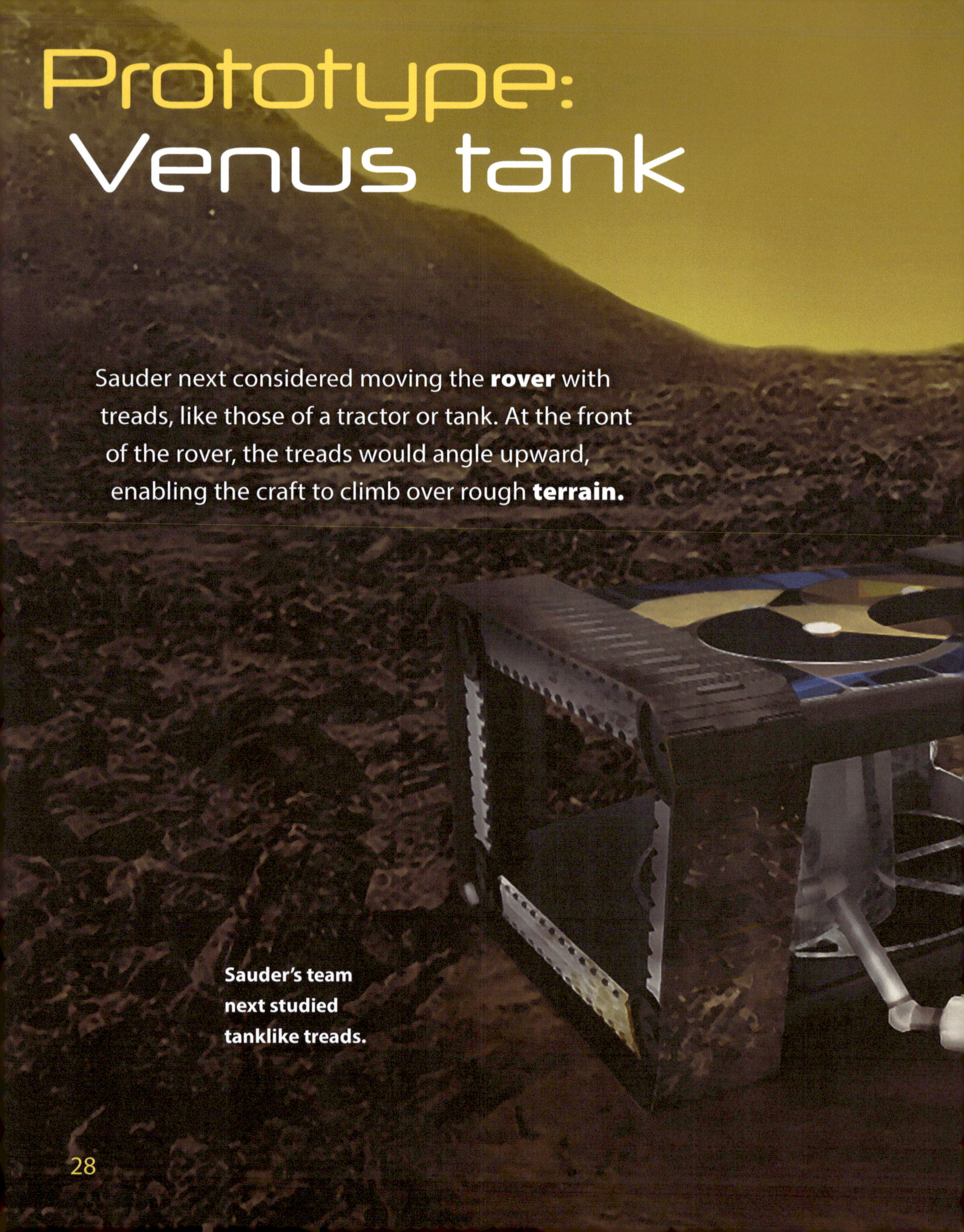

Sauder's team next studied tanklike treads.

Also, the treads could run around the entire
rover, from top to bottom. In fact, such a rover
would have no particular top or bottom. Faced
with an obstacle that could not be climbed, the
rover would simply flip over and set out in a new
direction—eliminating the need for electronic
systems to detect and avoid obstacles.

Sauder and his team ran into problems with
this approach during testing. The rover could
get stuck if it hit an obstacle between its treads.
The rover would need some kind of obstacle-
avoidance system after all. But then, what was
the point of having a flippable design?

Inventor feature:
Move fast, fail often

Sauder's background in entrepreneurship has given him a unique approach to **rover** design. Sauder favors testing out as many designs as possible, determining if they work, and discarding or improving upon them. It is a fast-moving approach inspired by the world of business, where beating your competitors to market can make the difference between success and failure. Sauder recalls some advice another **engineer,** Justin Koch, gave him when they were working at a startup company:

> When you're in a race with other companies, the one that builds the most **prototypes** wins. —Jonathan

Sauder's team is not directly competing with others, but this approach allows them to efficiently use their limited resources to develop HAR-V. There are lots of space exploration mission concepts out there. Using prototypes to prove an idea can work gives a mission concept an edge in being selected for further development.

Another element of Sauder's design strategy is recruiting a diverse team of people with different backgrounds. As shown by his collaboration with Theo Jansen, such diversity can provide unique perspectives. Sauder is also working with *horologists* (clockmakers) to create tiny gears and springs for HAR-V.

Working on anything challenging requires assembling the right team of people. —Jonathan

Prototype: How many wheels?

With legs and treads ruled out, Sauder turned to wheels. He first considered the six-wheeled system used on NASA's Mars **rovers.** These rovers rely on a *rocker-bogey suspension system.* In such a system, the wheels bob and bounce somewhat independently, enabling the rover to safely climb over obstacles.

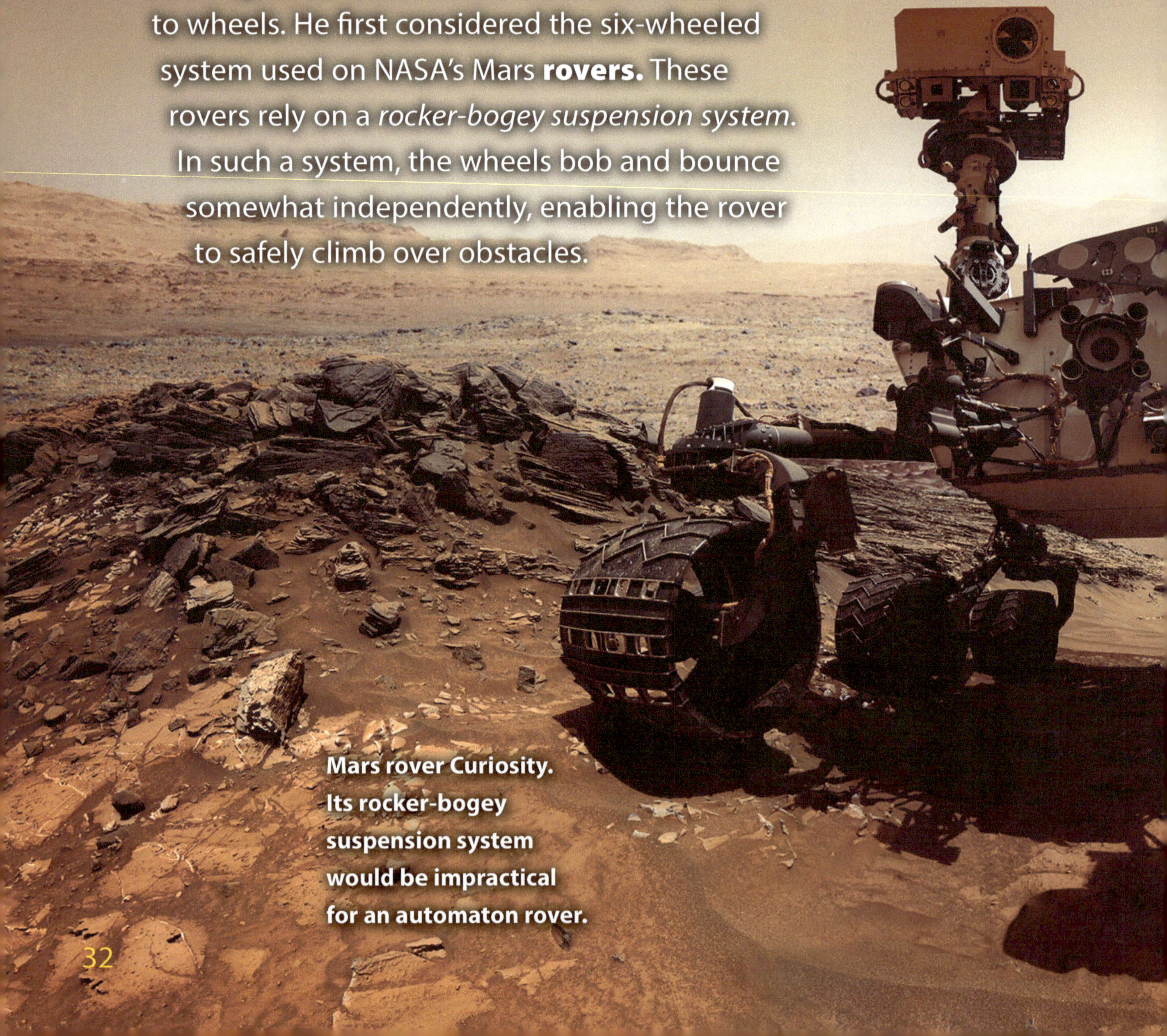

Mars rover Curiosity. Its rocker-bogey suspension system would be impractical for an automaton rover.

However, a rocker-bogey suspension system requires each wheel to be powered separately. On Mars, this is easily done with electric motors. But Venus is too hot for electric motors to operate efficiently. HAR-V's power will have to be transferred mechanically from the wind turbine directly to the wheels. It would be much too difficult to distribute power in this way to six separate wheels bouncing around in a rocker-bogey suspension system.

Through extensive testing, Sauder settled on a low-slung, four-wheeled design. Four big, *compliant* (flexible) tires will absorb the smaller bumps. With this design, HAR-V will be able to climb moderate slopes without tipping over, even when buffeted by wind gusts.

Mechanical bumper

HAR-V still needs some way to sense and avoid obstacles, so it can keep rolling across Venus's surface. Sauder has devised a way to do this mechanically, without any electronic **sensors.**

The **rover** will be equipped with a special front bumper. Any obstacle too tall to climb will hit the bumper, throwing a mechanical switch within the rover. This switch triggers a series of gear changes, causing the rover to back up a little, turn slightly, and move forward again. All of this is done with mechanical switches, gears, and axles, with no need for electrical power. If the obstacle is large, the rover will simply repeat the process each time it bumps into the obstacle until it has turned enough to avoid it.

To keep HAR-V from driving in circles, Sauder plans on using the wind direction of Venus as a mechanical compass. A true compass wouldn't work on Venus. But the wind tends to blow in one of two directions. If the rover keeps track of the wind direction with its wind turbine, it will take a zigzagging route across the planet.

Illustration of latest HAR-V
design, showing wind turbine,
four compliant tires, and
mechanical front bumper.

Hybrid
design

When Sauder first began to think about his **rover,** he envisioned a spacecraft powered entirely by **clockwork,** with no electric power or electronic parts. He even imagined a way for his rover to transmit data without the use of electronics. The craft would make use of a moveable reflector to relay data to an **orbiting** satellite, in much the same way that a person stranded in the wilderness might use a mirror to signal a passing airplane.

It was a worthy dream, but Sauder's team eventually determined that the system would transmit data at frustratingly slow speeds. It would also be impossible to gather certain

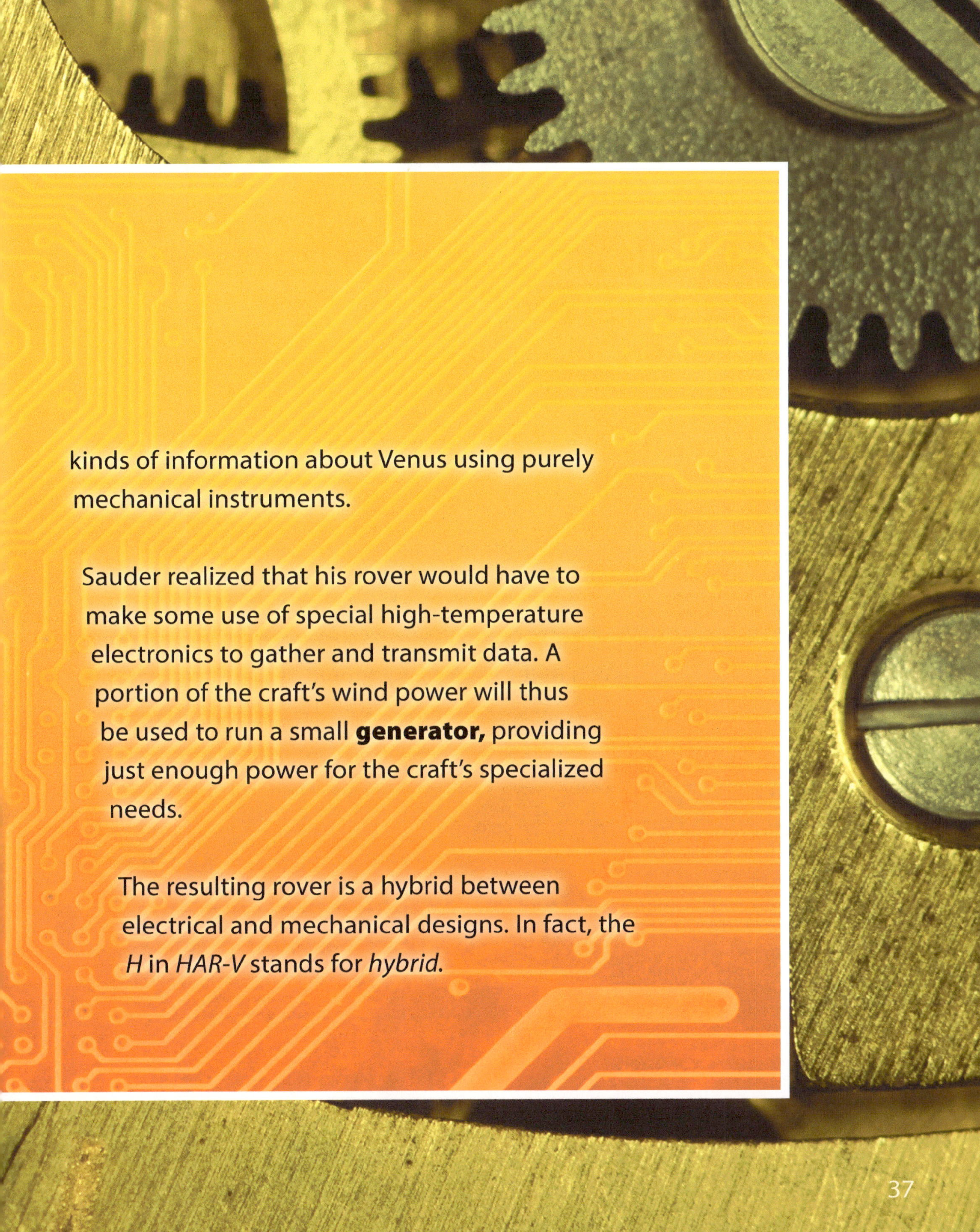

kinds of information about Venus using purely mechanical instruments.

Sauder realized that his rover would have to make some use of special high-temperature electronics to gather and transmit data. A portion of the craft's wind power will thus be used to run a small **generator,** providing just enough power for the craft's specialized needs.

The resulting rover is a hybrid between electrical and mechanical designs. In fact, the *H* in *HAR-V* stands for *hybrid*.

Inventor feature:
Building a better booster

Sauder has worked on a variety of projects in his career—from toys to satellites!

While working toward his master's degree, he served as an intern at the company Mattel, maker of Hot Wheels toy cars and tracks. There, he tackled a problem with battery-powered devices called boosters, which use a pair of spinning wheels to fling the cars faster along the tracks. The boosters would slow after launching a car, taking a second or two to regain full speed. If another car was following too close behind, it might not be boosted fast enough to make it through the whole circuit.

> **With the first car, the booster would slow down a little bit. With the second car, it would slow even more. The third car wouldn't get very much speed going through the booster at all, and it would fall off the track.** —Jonathan

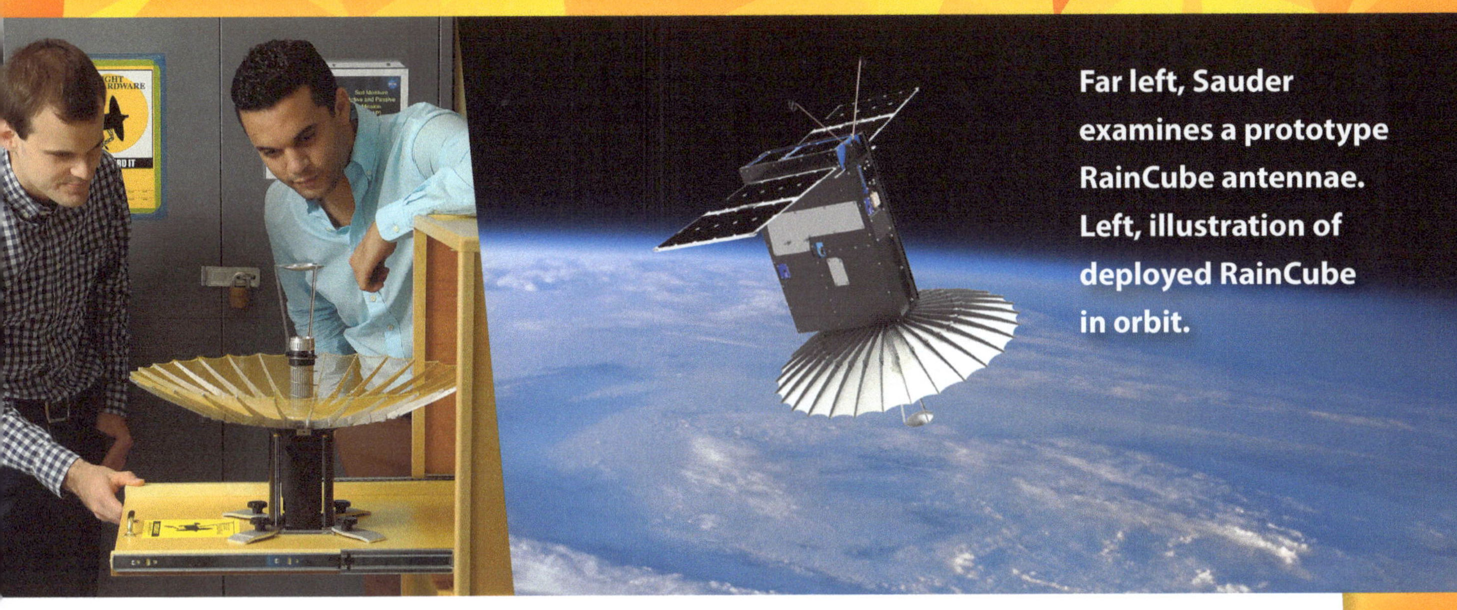

Far left, Sauder examines a prototype RainCube antennae. Left, illustration of deployed RainCube in orbit.

After extensive testing, Sauder determined that a device called the positive thermal controller (PTC) was slowing the booster. PTC's are included in many battery-powered toys to prevent the batteries from overheating. But Sauder determined that even without a PTC, the booster's batteries could not overheat. Removing the PTC improved the booster's performance by 60 percent.

Recently, Sauder served as the lead mechanical **engineer** for RainCube, a CubeSat designed to measure precipitation. CubeSats are tiny satellites designed to hitch a ride into space alongside larger craft. The usual size for a satellite measuring precipitation is about that of a small car. Sauder and his team managed to pack everything they needed into a satellite the size of a loaf of bread.

Testing
HAR-V

How do we know HAR-V will work in the extreme conditions of Venus?

Sauder's lead team member in developing HAR-V, Evan Hilgemann, has created a clock out of heat-resistant metals that can keep accurate time in a high-temperature oven. This shows that clockwork devices could be made to operate with precision on Venus. It's not just a neat experiment—the clock itself could also

Computer-generated projection of Venus's surface

be used in future **landers.** Such a clock might turn on
the lander periodically, conserving battery power and
extending the craft's life.

The next test for HAR-V will be the closest the **rover** can
get to Venus on Earth. The Jet Propulsion Laboratory
maintains a large chamber called the Venus Materials Test
Facility (VMTF). Like a giant pressure cooker, the VMFT
can recreate the intense temperatures and pressures on
the surface of Venus. Soon, a stainless-steel **prototype** of
HAR-V will attempt to drive the length of the VMTF, bump
into the end of the chamber, and back up.

**HAR-V prototype
makes a practice
run in the VMTF.**

Inventor feature:
Contests

As a child, Sauder loved entering contests for young inventors. He would sketch out a design for a new invention and mail it in. Once, he won a contest and was awarded an inventor's kit containing gears and motors, furthering his interest in **engineering.** Sauder is now using contests to help develop HAR-V.

" We're all learning here, and we're at the edge of doing new things for the first time. So, what's unique is that we can open this up to the maker community for ideas as to how to accomplish these things. " —Jonathan

Makers are modern-day tinkerers, modifying existing devices and inventing new ones. Some are professional engineers. But many are hobbyists working out of basements, garages, and other home workshops.

Sauder held a contest to get ideas for how the **rover** could detect obstacles and steep slopes on Venus without using electronic sensors.

This prototype featuring a mechanical bumper was designed by the Latvian company KOB ART.

Entrants were tasked with designing a mechanical bumper that could trigger the rover to switch gears and reverse if it encountered a large rock or steep slope.

❝ Challenges such as this are something that makers can directly relate to, understand, and get involved in from the start, unlike much of spacecraft engineering, which requires a lot of specific knowledge. ❞ —Jonathan

Sauder has developed several contest ideas to help solve HAR-V's engineering challenges, including developing a mechanical device to record data, coming up with a simple gear to mechanically reverse the rover, and designing a mechanical eye.

Jonathan Sauder and his team

Jonathan Sauder (right) and Evan Hilgemann in front of the Venus test chamber.

Intern Sean Dunphy

Intern Tonya Beatty

Industrial designer Jessie Kawata

Glossary

aerospace the field of science, technology, and industry dealing with the flight of rockets and spacecraft through the atmosphere or the space beyond it.

atmosphere the mass of gases that surrounds a planet.

carbon dioxide a colorless, odorless gas present in the atmospheres of many planets, including Earth.

clockwork a device that operates through the use of round gears, often powered by a coiled spring.

engineer a person who uses scientific principles to design structures, such as bridges and skyscrapers, machines, and all sorts of products.

exoplanet (extrasolar planet) a planet that orbits a star other than the sun.

generator a machine that changes mechanical energy into electricity.

lander a spacecraft designed to land on a planet, moon, or other body in space.

mass the amount of matter something contains.

orbit a looping path around an object in space; the condition of circling a massive object in space under the influence of the object's gravity.

orbiter a spacecraft designed to orbit a planet or other object in space.

probe a rocket, satellite, or other uncrewed spacecraft carrying scientific instruments, to record or report back information about space.

prototype a functional experimental model of an invention.

radiation energy given off in the form of waves or tiny particles of matter.

rover a lander designed to move about for surface exploration.

sensor a device that detects heat, light, or some other phenomenon, producing an electric signal.

solar system the sun and everything that travels around it, including Earth and all the other planets and their moons.

surface pressure the pressure on a planet's surface caused by the weight of the overlying atmosphere.

terrain an area of land, usually used when referring to the land's natural surface features.

turbine a device turned by the movement of a fluid—for example, the wind—to produce mechanical energy.

Inventor challenge: Titan rover

Jonathan Sauder came up with fresh ideas for exploring Venus's harsh surface with his HAR-V rover. Try your hand at designing a rover for another solar system body with a strange surface: Titan, the large moon of Saturn.

STEP 1 — Think about the challenge

Make a list of things you want to learn about Titan. Be sure to include questions needed to design a successful rover, such as atmospheric thickness and surface makeup. Gather information from reliable sources, such as World Book or NASA's website. Record answers to questions as you find them. As you read, write down questions about Titan that scientists would like answered, as well as any more of your own questions.

Create your prototype

Take a look at your list. The unanswered questions will be what you are designing your rover to find out. Think back to how Jonathan discarded all common ideas of what a rover should be to create the best design for Venus's harsh landscape. Be sure to do the same as you come up with your design. Does your rover even need wheels?

Share your design

Remember how Jonathan got advice on his first rover prototype from the artist Theo Jansen. Share your design with friends, classmates, or teachers. See what they think could be improved. If possible, share your design with engineers and scientists and ask for their input.

Grow your idea

Ask the people who gave you advice to help you revise your prototype. Perhaps someone with a special skill or interest can design a specific part, much like in Jonathan's contests. Then, incorporate these new designs into your prototype. Repeat until your rover is ready for launch!

Index

www.ingramcontent.com/pod-product-compliance
Lightning Source LLC
Chambersburg PA
CBHW042152030726
47599CB00004B/714